The Adventures of Detective Riah

Written by Tara Eddins

Illustrated by Nadeem Ch.

Edited by Eva Myrick, MSCP

THE ADVENTURES OF
DETECTIVE RIAH

The Adventures of Detective Riah

Just like many toddlers, Riah was seeking to gain her independence.

This included feeding herself, learning how to play with toys on her own, imitating mommy mixing and stirring in bowls and pots while playing in her toddler kitchen.

She loved getting praise for putting her dirty diapers in the trash and getting her own shoes when it was time to go outside and play (even though she would put on rainboots on a sunny day).

Waking up that morning, mommy gathered Riah, went to the bathroom, and started their morning routine. They started by brushing their teeth…although Riah did not like mommy to be fumbling around in her mouth. She wanted to brush her own teeth. Riah really liked the sweet strawberry flavor of kids' toothpaste. "Brush, don't swallow, spit." She brushed some more, then spit and rinsed with water. A small amount of kiddy mouthwash went "swoosh, swoosh, swoosh."

Riah could hear these instructions in her head as she brushed her teeth. It was at this moment Riah thought, "Could there be danger in this?" Riah knew she would need to investigate which would call for her detective gear. After bath time and getting Riah dressed, mommy left Riah's room to start breakfast.

Riah peeped down the hall toward the kitchen. She could see mommy at the stove cooking. Riah then turned her attention toward the opposite end of the hallway, where she could see the bathroom door closed. She knew daddy was taking his turn at bathroom time and getting ready for work.

Back in Riah's room, she turned all her attention to the toy box. Out with the dolls, the tea set, Minnie Mouse purse, the ABC Elephant, and other noise makers until she reached her detective gear which included a detective hat, her magnifying glass, and her brown detective coat.

She heard mom calling for her to eat breakfast. Out she came. Mommy just laughed, picked her up, and put her in the highchair. *No top of course that's for babies, my chair pulls right up to the table so I can eat just like the big people.* Daddy came out just in time, right when Riah reached for a strawberry, her favorite fruit. "Wait" mommy said, "We have to pray first." After prayer, Riah reached for a strawberry, and mommy encouraged her to use a fork or spoon. Riah chose a fork. It took her a few times, but she finally got her sausage on the fork. Daddy warned her to blow her food first. Riah just wanted to eat, but then her detective alarms went off.

She questioned, *Could there be danger in my food?* Grabbing her magnifying glass and looking at her food, she could see white steam. *Daddy warned, we must blow our food so that it's not too hot and we don't burn our mouth.* Even though mommy let her food cool off before giving it to her, Daddy still wanted Riah to learn to be aware. Riah blew each bite of eggs and sausage before eating them. Riah also remembered there could be danger in using adult utensils, like a fork. *We can stick our self with the sharp edges or stick a spoon too far in our mouth. Whoa danger avoided,* she thought.

After breakfast and back on the floor, Riah was still in detective mode and scanning the home for potential dangers. Looking around the living room, she noticed her car was plugged in. She thought she would ride around and look for danger. Riah got closer to the car, and was about to pull the plug from the electrical switch, when she heard her mother say, "Riah no, you could hurt yourself." Just like that Riah stopped, looking confused. Mommy continued, "You don't ever pull anything out, or plug anything in, and most definitely never stick anything in these sockets, you can get electrocuted." Although Riah did not know what that meant, she understood danger and backed away. Minutes later, Riah saw her mother putting plastic covers in all the open electrical plugs. *Whoa another danger avoided*, Riah thought.

Mommy turned off Riah's favorite educational programs. As interested as Riah was, she also thought there could be more danger and she had to find it. She found herself in the kitchen, and remembered mommy and daddy in the cabinets getting pots and pans, sprays, food, and sponges. Riah thought she would look in the cabinets to see what she could find. She opened the cabinet and found a white spray bottle with a picture on the side that looked like a picture of a Halloween skull and bones.

Starting to get somewhat annoyed, mom yelled out, "Put that down!" Dropping the bottle to the floor and jumping back after being startled, Riah asked, "Why?" Mom responded, "That is a cleaning chemical that can be poisonous and very painful if you get it into your eyes or mouth. You can get very sick, and we would have to take you to the hospital." Riah realized she had just discovered another danger.

Mom instructed Riah back to the living room, where Riah heard another familiar sound. The ice cream truck! She ran straight for the door. Pressing against the door, she yelled back to her mother, "Ice cream mommy!" Watching as the truck slowly passed by her house, she saw the neighborhood kids running to the truck. Riah knew she had to get to the truck too. She tried to use her magnifying glass to reach up and get the door handle to open. Mom could hear noises coming from the front door. Peeping around the corner, she said, "Stop that before you fall out the door." *Fall out the door*, Riah thought, *How can there be danger in wanting to get ice cream?* She thought about her favorite superman ice cream and how wonderful it tasted. But hearing this put her back into detective mode. With a very concerned face, she continued to listen to mommy explain how she could fall out the door and hurt herself if she fell down the steps, or that she could have gotten hit by a car that did not see her if she ran out in the street after the ice cream truck, or could be bitten by a dog. "You could have gotten the door open and let a stranger in the house that could have hurt us." Riah was astonished. She had no idea it was so much danger in getting ice cream.

Mom took Riah out and got her a superman ice cream cone. Back in the house and out of danger Riah, sat on the couch eating her ice cream and thinking about all the danger she learned about today. Feeling exhausted, she thought *surely there is no danger in taking a nap.* She angled herself where she could see the TV and noticed her eyes getting heavy. In no time, Riah was asleep.